Dahlias

cultivation · care · inspiration

Ulrika Grönlund

Hardie Grant

QUADRILLE

Contents

'LABYRINTH'

Introduction

It's July. In the garden there's an explosion of dahlias in the raised beds in front of the orangery. Every day one dahlia after another bursts into bloom, filling the garden with colour, shape, buzzing bees, flitting butterflies, and a superabundance of flowers. No other flower can match the dahlia and thanks to the 64,000 registered varieties, everyone can find a colour or shape to fall in love with. A single tuber planted in the spring will become a plant that produces an abundance of flowers for several months – usually from July until the first frost. A dream come true for anyone that wants a host of blooms in the beds and loves cut flowers.

Dahlias are easy to grow, and if the plants are provided with good conditions, a dahlia growers' biggest problem will be finding room for all the new varieties.

Welcome to the fantastic world of dahlias, and hopefully a lifelong passion for flowers!

Ulrika Grönlund
Sweden

Instagram: @dahliafarmen and @ulrikagronlund1

'LINDAS' BABY'

'CAFÉ AU LAIT'

The history of the dahlia

The dahlia originally comes from the mountainous regions of Mexico and Guatemala, where it grows in meadows and alongside roads, just like our wild flowers do in Sweden. Dahlias thrive on volcanic slopes several thousand metres above sea level, at an average temperature of 15°C (59°F).

The Aztecs grew dahlias as medicinal plants, as the tubers could reduce swelling, relieve stomach ache and alleviate epilepsy. The hollow stems were also used as water tubes and pipes, and as containers when out hunting.

Wealthy Aztecs also grew dahlias together with fruit, vegetables, ornamental plants and herbs.

In 1492 when Columbus and his crew arrived in the Americas, the Spaniards were greatly impressed by the Aztecs' exotic gardens. More and more Europeans visited what they called 'Nueva España', and the Spaniards began to write down and categorize the vegetation of the area.

At the end of the sixteenth century drawings of three different dahlia varieties, with both single and double flowers, were sent to Madrid. In 1789 a boatload of Mexican plants arrived at Madrid's botanical gardens, where the cultivation of dahlias began and the flowers were named after the Swedish botanist, Anders Dahl. By 1800 dahlias were being sent to botanical gardens all over Europe. Cross-breeding of dahlias gave rise to many new varieties and to different colours and shapes, and so interest in dahlias has spread all over the world. There are now over 64,000 different named varieties.

Caring for your dahlias

Dahlias are relatively undemanding; they don't need much attention in order to thrive and deliver flowers month after month. The better the conditions you give them the easier it will be to achieve really beautiful, opulent plants. As dahlia growers tend to buy more and more varieties every year, lifting and storing them over the winter can become quite a challenge. But most people find the effort worthwhile for the months of pleasure the flowers provide. If you don't want to spend time digging the tubers up and storing them over the winter you can simply buy new ones every year.

'WINE EYED JILL', 'OTTO'S THRILL' AND 'NICK SR'.

Soil and fertilizers

Get to know your soil

Soil is fundamental to all horticulture, and dahlias are no exception. The soil is one of the most important components when it comes to achieving healthy, thriving plants that will flower for several months. Get to know your soil and create a sustainable cycle whereby the nutrition the dahlias take up is returned every year in the form of compost, grass clippings, leaves and fertilizer.

Good soil is loose and rich in nutrition and humus. Humus is made up of biological particles from decomposing plants and animals, and it contains lots of nutrition and moisture. 'Loose' means airy and light, so oxygen can get to the roots and they can grow unhindered. Whether you have light sandy soil, heavy clay soil or hard dry soil, dahlias will be grateful for compost and decomposed manure, which you should mix in with a spade pushed about 40 cm (16 in) down into the soil. It's hard to say how much you should use, as this depends on the quality of the original soil, but it should make the soil loose and easy to dig. I put three to four bags of cow manure into each of my own 2 x 2 m (6½ x 6½ ft) growing beds (see pages 138–139) every spring. In the autumn, when the dahlias have been lifted and the stems cut off, I dig in small batches of flowers, leaves and cut-up stems – ideally together with grass clippings and fallen leaves. Worms help disperse the compost, loosen the soil and excellently fertilize it with their vermicast (excrement) until it's time for planting again.

Fertilizers

As well as basal dressing (fertilizer applied to the soil before planting), dahlias need a little TLC during the season, so they will flower to the full from early summer until the first frost, and grow into strong plants that are resistant to various forms of attack. Nitrogen (N), phosphorus (P) and potassium (K) are the three nutrients most important to growth in the garden. NPK constitute food for plants, and are comparable to carbohydrates, fat and protein for humans. Nitrogen is a nutrient that supports leaf development, making plants green and luxuriant. A lack of nitrogen weakens plants and makes them pale in colour, but too much nitrogen can make dahlias grow lots of leaves but few flowers. Phosphorus promotes the plants' root development, bud formation and flowering. Potassium increases resistance to disease.

There's an abundance of fertilizers available, and both liquid plant food and pellets work with dahlias. Liquid food is preferable when growing in pots, whilst pellets are easier to spread in big flower beds. The distribution of NPK varies from one fertilizer to another – choose one best suited to flowering plants. How often you need to fertilize depends on the basal dressing and the specific soil you have. Experiment to see what works best in your garden. I do maintenance fertilizing once every three weeks, from the dahlias' first flowering through to the beginning of the autumn.

Watering

Dahlias love water, but don't like standing in it as the tubers may rot. When you've planted the tubers in the soil outside you can hold back on watering them until the first shoots begin to appear. Let the soil dry out between waterings. The bigger the plant the more water it will need. How much and how often you need to water depends on the type of soil you have, where you live and what the weather's like. Dahlias planted in pots need regular watering.

Deadheading

This means regularly cutting off fading flowers together with their stems. Deadheading stimulates new flowering and will make your plants look fresh and attractive. If you want to collect seeds from your dahlias, don't cut the flowers off; instead allow them to fade and form seed capsules.

Indoor precultivation

If you have a lot of dahlias you might consider whether precultivation – early growing indoors – for a few weeks of earlier flowering is worth the trouble, given that they flower for several months in any case. If you have problems with slugs and snails, who tend to like nibbling the tender dahlia shoots, precultivation is definitely worthwhile. It gives the plant a head start, away from slugs and snails, while developing. Early growing indoors at room temperature usually starts in spring, depending on where you live. Starting too early just makes for tall, leggy plants. A lot of people start plants into growth in soil-filled plastic bags, but keep in mind that the whole tuber must be covered in soil. Personally I prefer early growing in pots as they're more stable and easier to move when it's time to take them out for hardening-off in the sun – but on the other hand they do take up more space.

Pinching

Opinions on this issue are divided. Some people think pinching plants early makes them bushier and more stable. Others, however, think the opposite; namely that if you top dahlias too many side shoots will form and fewer flowers will develop as the plants will not receive as much sunlight as taller plants, and so will become unstable. Experiment and find out what works best for you.

Planting and labelling

Position

Choose a sunny spot for your dahlias, as they love the sun and generally need at least six hours' sunlight every day in order to flower and develop optimally. I've tried growing them in semi-shade with 3–4 hours' sunlight a day, and the result was later flowering and fewer flowers.

Whether or not you've started growing indoors, the tubers must be planted at a depth of about 10–15 cm (4–6 in). Any less deep, and they'll be unstable and will lean in various directions. The month and day you plant will be governed by the temperature and when the risk of frost has passed – all depending on where you live. In the event of a bout of frost after you've planted out your small dahlias you can cover them with a row cover or garden fabric until the risk has passed. If you've planted tubers they will cope with a few frosty nights, as the soil will protect them.

Height

You need to be aware of how high your dahlias will grow. If you're planting against a wall or hedge the tallest should be positioned right at the back and the shortest right at the front. This is so the tall ones don't put the shorter ones in the shade, as they would then flower very poorly or not at all. If you have a square or round flower bed, the tallest dahlias should be planted in the middle.

'PINELANDS PRINCESS' AT MAGNOLIA IN NOSSEBRO.

DIVIDED TUBERS READY FOR PLANTING.

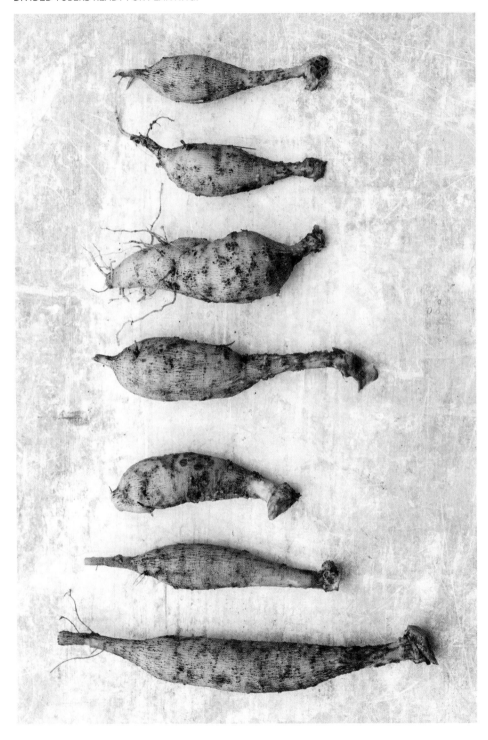

Distance between plants

You'll find out the spread of your dahlias after the first season, and will notice that some varieties become huge and spread out both vertically and horizontally. These varieties need more space than the smaller ones. The spread and height can also vary depending on the number of hours of sunlight, the soil, the fertilizer and watering. A distance of approximately 40–60 cm (1^1/$_3$–2 ft) between plants is usually about right – for shorter varieties about 40 cm (16 in) and for taller ones 60 cm (24 in). Planting them too close together will mean that the lack of light will force the plants to grow taller and less stable, and they will need more tying in. There will also be fewer flowers, and diseases such as mildew will thrive in the cramped and warm conditions.

Planting in pots

Planting dahlias in pots works very well. Don't choose very tall varieties; ideally select ones that grow to about 1 m (3 ft) in height, as they will cope best when it's windy and rainy, even though they may still need some form of support, such as canes. Dahlias thrive in ordinary gardening soil mixed with a few litres of cow manure, and the pots should be solid and at least 50–60 cm (19–23 in) in diameter, so the tubers can develop roots that can spread and not be cramped. If you grow plants in pots you must water them often and feed them about once every three weeks.

Tying, support and labelling

Dahlias are more resistant than you might think and can withstand a lot of wind and rain. But when a storm is on its way it's advisable to tie your plants to a support. So when you plant your tubers it's wise to insert canes or iron supports at the same time, so the tubers don't get damaged when you stick the canes in later on. Big, tall varieties may need several canes, whilst short ones won't need tying up at all as they're compact and stable in terms of their growth. Curved plant supports, which are often used for bushes or peonies, are perfect if some of your dahlias are starting to hang down over beds or borders. And don't forget to label your plants.

When you dig up your dahlias in late autumn you'll be surprised by the number of tubers that have formed, and by how different they look depending on the variety. Regardless of size, after dividing each tuber should comprize of a body, a neck and a crown.

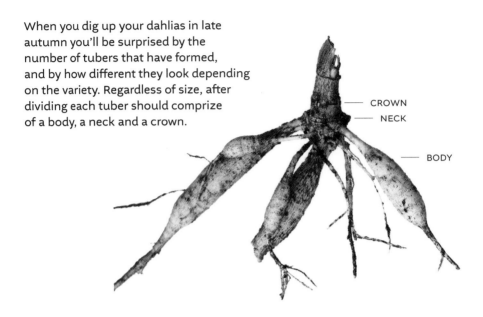

CROWN
NECK
BODY

RAY FLORETS

DISC FLORETS

BRACTS

CROSS-SECTION OF A DAHLIA

Propagating from tubers, cuttings or seeds

Tubers

The most common way of propagating dahlias is by dividing the tubers, which you can do in autumn or spring. An advantage of dividing in the spring is that the little dark eyes, which are the new shoots, will be starting to grow from the tubers, making it easier to see where to divide. Each divided tuber must have a body and a neck, and needs to have a little of the so-called crown left, as this is where the growth points will be. A tuber without any growth points will never produce any shoots. When you divide dahlias using a knife or secateurs, you leave an open wound. Let this heal and dry before planting or storing for winter, otherwise there's a risk of mould forming. With some divided tubers it may be hard to determine whether any of the crown is present. You can push these tubers down into a pot filled with soil, and wait and see. Is it necessary to divide tubers? No, not after the first or second year. But as the root clumps get bigger and bigger, so the plant's ability to flower deteriorates, and the tubers will become so compact that you'll have to divide them using an axe or split them with a spade.

If you divide your dahlias in the autumn it's a good idea to first wash the soil off the tubers. When doing so in the spring you can just brush away the dried soil before dividing them. All root clumps look different, and you can start by halving them using secateurs or a sharp knife. You can also try dividing them manually, by carefully jiggling them then breaking them. Then in turn divide the halves, and continue until you've divided them all. Lastly cut off the thin adhesive roots.

'APPLE BLOSSOM' HAS AN OPEN DISC AND IS A FAVOURITE OF BEES.

Cuttings

Cuttings should be taken as early in the spring as possible. Wake up the tubers you want cuttings from as early as the very end of winter, as it shifts into spring, by planting them in small pots so that some of the neck and crown protrude.

Put the pots somewhere as light as possible, at room temperature, and wait a few weeks until the green shoots are approximately 10 cm (4 in) long. Ideally you should have access to grow lights, but otherwise try putting the pots on a windowsill. Cut the cutting off at the base using a sharp knife or scalpel, but make sure you don't remove all of the eye from the root. The highest concentration of natural root-promoting hormone is found at the growth point – or the 'eye' – between the old growth and where a new shoot is to form. Remove the lowest leaves on the cutting and maybe dip the cutting in a chemical rooting hormone.

Set the cutting in a seed and cutting soil mix or light soil mixed with sand or LECA balls, and make sure the former location of the lowest leaf pair is covered by soil. Water and carefully press in, so the cutting makes good contact with the soil. Allow the soil to dry out between waterings, otherwise the cutting may easily rot.

Cuttings can also be taken from a mature plant at a later stage, by cutting off the top of a stem. Remove the lowest leaf pairs before planting. If you take a cutting later than mid-spring it may not manage to flower and produce tubers.

Cuttings must be placed in a light, warm spot, but not in direct sunlight – ideally with a plastic bag on top for a week or so, until they've taken. Water sparingly. Make sure air can get in by piercing a few holes in the bag. Gardening centres also sell mini-greenhouses.

It takes approximately six to eight weeks for cuttings to produce their own roots and become ready for planting out. Cuttings need to be acclimatized to the sun before planting out in the growing site, for a few hours a day for about a week.

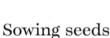

REMOVE THE LOWER LEAVES OF THE CUTTING.

DRIED DAHLIA SEEDS CAN BE STORED IN ORDINARY COFFEE FILTERS.

Sowing seeds

A dahlia grown from seed will not be genetically identical to its parent plants. The embryo in the seed differs from the parent plant genetically, and the new flowers that develop from the seedling will thus not look the same as those of the plant the seed was taken from. This means that if you want a variety identical to the one you've grown you must save the tubers or take cuttings, not propagate with seeds.

It's fun to buy a few packets of dahlia seeds and then excitedly wait and see what the flowers will be like! About a month before the last frost – though this varies from year to year – it's time to sow your dahlia seeds. If you sow too early, and there is too much time between sowing and planting out the dahlias, they will become tall, leggy and fragile.

Fill small pots with sowing soil and gently press it down a little with your fingers. Then make a small hole with a fingertip, press the seed in and cover with a thin layer of soil. You can set several seeds in the same pot, but if you notice that all the seeds are taking, you'll need to transfer the plants to their own small pots so you don't damage the roots, which tend to grow into each other if they're too close together. Water carefully, ideally using a rose attachement to start with. Put them in a warm and sunny place in the greenhouse or on a windowsill. You can cover the pots with plastic so a moist greenhouse climate forms, but the seeds will usually grow regardless.

When your small plants have got bigger, and there is no more risk of a frost, they will need to be acclimatized to the sun for a few hours a day for about a week before planting them out in the growing site. Be particularly thorough when getting rid of slugs and snails now, as they love the small, tender shoots.

Pollination creates new varieties

One of the reasons why dahlias are so popular is the fact that there are such a huge number of varieties. Creation of these varieties through cross-breeding has been possible as dahlias have eight sets of chromosomes, that is 64 chromosomes in total, whilst most other flowers have far fewer – often just two sets. This allows an infinite number of dahlia crossings.

You can try creating completely new varieties of dahlia by selecting two different varieties of dahlia as parent plants. For those wishing to give it a go there are books on reproductive biology, as well as informative YouTube videos. The following is a basic guide.

To prevent insects getting in there first, the flowers you want to cross should be covered with small mesh bags or cut-off nylon stockings before they have matured. The flowers contain both male and female organs. Cut off a flower with pollen-covered stamens and rub it against the parent plant's pistils. Repeat the procedure on day two, then wait for the seeds to form. This must be done when both the male and female flowers are mature.

At the end of the season you can also save seeds from your own dahlias that bees have pollinated – maybe the variety you're growing will be the next big seller! Allow the plant to finish blooming, leave the buds on for a few weeks, then harvest the seed capsules and dry them indoors. When they're completely dry and brown you can pick out the seeds with your fingers then keep them dry in a coffee filter, for example. You can label them with the name of the variety the seeds came from, but the new plants' flowers will be a surprise, as it's the bees who will have done the pollination. Very exciting!

Lifting and winter storage

The first frosty nights

If you get the odd early frosty night in autumn where you live, you can cover the dahlias with garden fabric overnight, so they will hopefully be able to flower for a few more weeks before the onset of persistent sub-zero temperatures. If you've not already labelled each variety with its name and height, make sure you do so before the frost arrives, as it will be hard to identify the varieties afterwards.

When the frost has arrived and all the dahlias have become black overnight, it's time to start thinking about the tubers' dormancy and storage. The dahlias don't have to be dug up the same day, as the tubers are protected by the soil and will withstand more than you'd expect. It's best to wait a few weeks after the first frost. I've left tubers in place over the winter in areas with severe sub-zero temperatures, and they've coped with overwintering outdoors. This is not recommended for particularly cherished varieties, but it shows they're pretty resistant. The longer the dahlias remain in the soil, the more nutrition the tubers can take in. It's also a good idea to delay digging them up, as they form thick, protective shells in late autumn.

Lift the tubers with a fork or spade and shake off most of the soil. Bear in mind that they will have expanded underground, so dig well underneath them to avoid damaging them. If you do damage or cut into a tuber with the spade, allow the surface to dry out for a few days to prevent rot developing. Many people spread cinnamon over open cut surfaces to prevent fungal attack. When the tubers have been lifted, cut off the stems but leave 10 cm (4 in) remaining.

Frost-free winter storage

There are many different ways of storing dahlia tubers over winter – you'll need to adapt your storage to the space you have available. The optimal location will be frost-free, relatively dry and cool (4–7°C/39–44°F), e.g. a garage or storeroom. If these conditions are available, after lifting the tubers the easiest thing is to shake off most of the soil and then store them in ordinary plastic pots, paper bags or open trays. Bear in mind that the floor of a cold storeroom will tend to be moist, so store the tubers on shelves. Many people who grow in pots simply cut off the stem and store the whole pot with tuber and soil as it is. In the spring the tuber is taken out and divided, then planted in new soil.

If you can't provide these conditions you should nevertheless try to overwinter the tubers. If it's too warm the tubers may dry out, and if it's too moist they may rot. If the location is dry and warm a layer of soil can provide protection – wood shavings, sawdust, newspaper and peat can also be used. You can also store the tubers in a fridge at 4–7°C (39–44°F), without soil, divided and wrapped in cling film. All experienced dahlia growers have adapted their winter storage methods to their own environment, so there's not really any right or wrong way to do this. The main thing is that it works, and that the tubers survive the winter without freezing, going mouldy, or shrinking and drying out.

Pests and diseases

Although dahlias are highly resistant, like all plants they're vulnerable to pests and diseases. As long as you've not planted them too close together, they're in nutritious, well-cultivated soil and you water them regularly, the plants will be more resistant. Below are the most common pests and diseases.

Slugs and snails

Slugs and snails are many dahlia growers' nemesis, as these creatures love chomping tender dahlia shoots. Indoor precultivation is recommended if you have a lot of slugs and snails, as this gives the dahlias a head start. Remove the plant's lowest leaves, so that the slug's and snail's first taste is of the bitter stem, and they will hopefully go elsewhere. Raised beds make things harder for snails, as does regularly loosening the soil with a small hoe or spade, as this will make it more difficult for them to get around. You can also try eco-certified slug killers and organic slug control with nematodes, which are microscopic worms that kill slugs and snails. If you grow in pallet collars, there are special anti-snail edges available that they cannot get past. Otherwise, remove all the slugs and snails you can see and cut off slugs' heads with scissors or secateurs, as they reproduce fast.

Earwigs

Many people have problems with earwigs chewing both the flowers and the leaves. Earwigs are light-sensitive and seek out dark, moist places to reproduce. They're active at night and hide when it gets light. You can make your own traps by rolling up sheets of moistened corrugated cardboard, and they will creep inside. Attach the rolls of cardboard to a stick. You can also use upside-down flower pots, which you can fill with cloth, straw or corrugated cardboard. Empty all the traps in the morning, otherwise the earwigs will come back at night.

Aphids

Aphids are at their most active at the beginning of the dahlia season, disappearing almost completely later on. But they can do a great deal of damage in that time, weakening plants and inhibiting growth by sucking out sap. Sooty mould can start growing in the sticky honeydew aphids leave behind, preventing light from reaching the leaves. If you discover black blotches on the leaves you can try drying off the sooty mould. Aphids can also spread diseases from one plant to another.

You can try washing the stems, whilst removing the aphids with your thumb and index finger. They will return, but this is an environmentally friendly and effective method. You can also spray the aphids with a mixture of one part soap to 20 parts water. Another useful trick is smearing petroleum jelly on the stems. And ladybirds are aphids' natural enemies, so the more ladybirds the better! Lastly, if you can get rid of ants you'll have fewer aphids as ants milk aphids for their honeydew.

Thrips

Thrips are small insects – a few millimetres long – that suck sap from leaves. The leaf cells lose sap and are instead filled with air, creating a grey or silvery appearance. The leaves will eventually dry out and go brown. You can use the same soap dilution against thrips as that recommended for aphids above.

Mosaic virus

When dahlias are attacked by the mosaic virus the leaves develop light-green or yellow blotches. The leaves may also become twisted and the plant may stop growing. This infection principally comes from tubers, but is usually spread by aphids. These mosaic-like attacks can also be seen on potatoes, beetroot and tomatoes. Any plants affected should be dug up, and both the tubers and the stems should be discarded as combustible waste. It can be hard to judge whether a plant has succumbed to the mosaic virus or just has some deficiency that makes parts of the leaves go pale.

Mildew

If you see a white coating on the leaves your dahlias have probably been affected by mildew. The coating will sometimes be blotchy and sometimes the entire plant will be affected. Mildew is a fungus that can be caused by too much nitrogen fertilizer and dehydration, but also by plants being too close together or weakened by incorrect care which can reduce their resistance. Mildew usually appears relatively late in the season. There are fungicides containing nitrogen that can be sprayed on, but you should use these as a preventive procedure. As soon as you see any hint of a white coating you should pick off the leaves affected and then spray the rest of the plant, treating both sides of the leaves. Then spray again after it has rained, and be sure to water the plants. You can also try sprinkling wood ash over them, or treating them with bicarbonate of soda: 1–2 teaspoons of bicarbonate plus 1–2 teaspoons of rapeseed oil to 1 litre (2 pints) of water.

Leafy gall

Leafy gall is a bacterial disease caused by the bacterium *Rhodococcus fascians*. The disease is characterized by abnormal accumulations of small shoots, often close to ground level. Leafy gall is to be found in many soils and it can also attack several other plants, such as pelargoniums, chrysanthemums, sweet peas and strawberries. If you find a dahlia with leafy gall, dig it up and throw it in the waste bin – not in the compost. Clean the tools you used to dig up or cut down the sick plant, so the bacteria does not spread to other plants.

Crown gall

Crown gall is caused by the bacterium *Rhizobium radiobacter*. The bacterium enters the dahlia tubers or stems through wounds and stimulates the plant to produce growths known as galls, which can take various forms. Crown gall also attacks fruit trees, beetroot, sweet peas, phlox and begonias. If you find dahlias with crown gall they should be dug up and thrown in the waste bin – not in the compost. Clean your tools thoroughly. Grow potatoes for two years in succession exactly where the affected dahlia was to help rid the soil of the bacterium.

THE VARIOUS STAGES OF MILDEW.

Dahlia varieties

Here you will find over two hundred dahlia varieties, ranging from tiny pompom dahlias to huge decorative dahlias. Each variety is grouped by colour and below each photograph there's information on the variety's characteristics: the group it belongs to, as well as its height, flower diameter and stem length. Each variety was measured when the photograph was taken.

Varieties and classification

As a dahlia grower you should be aware that plants' characteristics can vary, depending on the conditions they're given. Temperatures, growing zones, watering and genetics are examples of parameters that play a role. The stem size can vary greatly in the same plant – as can the flower diameter and colour. In a number of varieties the colour of the flower can change considerably at the end of the season, when it gets colder. One example is 'Wine Eyed Jill', which at the beginning of the season has a lot of cerise in it. A month or so later the pink colour becomes softer, whilst at the same time a pastel yellow hue emerges, and by the end of the season, when the cold weather arrives, nearly all of the flowers will be light yellow. The height can also vary a lot in plants of the same variety. If you plant them too close together you may either get taller plants as a result of them struggling to reach the light, or smaller ones that don't flower well because it's too dark.

Most of the varieties in this book are relatively easy to get hold of, but there are some exceptions. It's difficult and expensive to import tubers from countries outside the EU as phytosanitary certificates are required, although some collectors have succeeded in importing tubers, which you can buy or acquire through exchange on various buying and selling websites.

Dahlias are classified according to flower size, colour, and shape.* The flowers are split into groups differently around the world, but in Sweden we divide the flowers into 7 different groups by size, 11 different groups by colour and 16 different groups by shape.

Size:
Giant – over 25 cm (10 in) in diameter
Large – 20–25 cm (8–10 in) in diameter
Medium – 15–20 cm (6–8 in) in diameter
Small – 10–15 in (4–6 in) in diameter
Miniature – under 10 cm (4 in) in diameter

The following applies to ball dahlias:
Miniature – 5–10 cm (2–4 in) in diameter
Pompom – under 5 cm (2 in) in diameter

Colour:

White

Yellow

Orange

Red, dark red

Pink

Lilac, lavender, mauve

Purple, violet

Bronze

Fiery red

Mixed-colour (where colours gradually blend into each other)

Multicoloured (where two or more colours can be clearly differentiated)

*Please note that for printing reasons the colour of the flowers on pages 38–133 slightly differs from their actual colour.

1. **Single-flowered dahlia**: The flower has a ring of eight ray florets, which may overlap with each other. The middle of the flower is an open disc.

2. **Anemone-flowering dahlia**: The flower has a single ring of ray florets surrounded by a group of closely-spaced tubular disc florets.

3. **Collarette dahlia**: The flower has a single ring of ray florets that are normally flat and can overlap with each other, plus an inner ring of small ray florets. It has an open disc.

4. **Peony dahlia**: It has several rings of ray florets around an open disc. The florets are flat or curled slightly inwards at the base, but can also be curled outwards towards the tip.

5. **Formal decorative dahlia**: The flowers are fully double. The ray florets are usually broad and curled slightly inwards at the base, and they end with a tip or indentation.

6. **Ball dahlias**: The flowers are fully double and ball-shaped or slightly flattened. The ray florets have rounded tips and form a spiral pattern.

7. **Pompom dahlia**: Fully double flowers in miniature size, under 5 cm (2 in) in diameter. The ray florets are curled inwards throughout their length and are rounded at the tip.

8. **Cactus dahlia**: The flowers are fully double and the ray florets are pointed and curled outwards for over 50 per cent of their length.

9. **Semi-cactus dahlia**: The flowers are fully double and the ray florets are pointed and curled outwards for 25 per cent to 50 per cent of their length.

10. **Miscellaneous dahlias**: All dahlias that do not fit into the other types.

11. **Laciniated dahlias**: Fully double flowers in which the ray florets have split, notched or fringed tips.

12. **Single orchid dahlia (star-shaped)**: The flowers have a single ring or ray florets around an open disc. The ray florets are slender and often curled inwards, but they can also be curled outwards.

13. **Double orchid dahlia**: The flowers are fully double and have broad, sparsely positioned ray florets that can be flat or slightly rolled inwards.

14. **Waterlily dahlia**: Fully double flowers with ray florets that are flat or slightly curved-in at the base.

15. **Informal decorative dahlia**: The flowers are perceived as being irregular and are fully double. The ray florets, which are flat or slightly curved inwards at the base, are also twisted and curled outwards.

16. **Large pompom dahlia**: The same shape as the ordinary pompom dahlia but with a diameter of 5–7.5 cm (2–3 in).

1. Ball dahlia
'Sweet Suzanne'
Flower size: 8–9 cm
(3¼–3½ in)
Height: 110 cm (43 in)
Stem: 30 cm (12 in)

2. Decorative dahlia
'Lady Darlene'
Flower size: 22 cm (8½ in)
Height: 120 cm (47 in)
Stem: 30 cm (12 in)

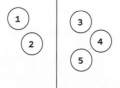

3. Decorative dahlia
'Seattle'
Flower size: 10 cm (4 in)
Height: 120 cm (47 in)
Stem: 10 cm (4 in)

4. Semi-cactus dahlia
'Shooting Star'
Flower size: 17 cm (6½ in)
Height: 130 cm (51 in)
Stem: 20–30 cm (8–12 in)

5. Ball dahlia
'Souvenir d'Été'
Flower size: 5 cm (2 in)
Height: 70 cm (27 in)
Stem: 10 cm (4 in)

6. Decorative dahlia
'Kelvin Floodlight'
Flower size: 20 cm (8 in)
Height: 80 cm (32 in)
Stem: 10–20 cm (4–8 in)

7. Decorative dahlia
'Hollyhill Lemon Ice'
Flower size: 15 cm (6 in)
Height: 100 cm (39 in)
Stem: 10 cm (4 in)

8. Decorative dahlia
'La Luna'
Flower size: 20–22 cm
(8–8½ in)
Height: 90 cm (36 in)
Stem: 20 cm (8 in)

9. Anemone-flowering dahlia
'Polka'
Flower size: 12 cm (5 in)
Height: 140 cm (55 in)
Stem: 20 cm (8 in)

10. Waterlily dahlia
'Pacific Ocean'
Flower size: 9 cm (3½ in)
Height: 90 cm (36 in)
Stem: 10 cm (4 in)

11. Pompom dahlia
'Kasasagi'
Flower size: 5 cm (2 in)
Height: 100 cm (39 in)
Stem: 10 cm (4 in)

12. Waterlily dahlia
'Orange Perception'
Flower size: 10 cm (4 in)
Height: 100 cm (39 in)
Stem: 10–20 cm (4–8 in)

13. Collarette dahlia
'Kelsey Annie Joy'
Flower size: 9 cm (3½ in)
Height: 110 cm (43 in)
Stem: 10–20 cm (4–8 in)

14
15
16
17
18
19

14. Single orchid dahlia (star-shaped)
'Honka'
Flower size: 12 cm (5 in)
Height: 100 cm (39 in)
Stem: 10–20 cm (4–8 in)

15. Double orchid dahlia
'Giraffe'
Flower size: 10–14 cm (4–5½ in)
Height: 90 cm (36 in)
Stem: 30 cm (12 in)

16. Pompom dahlia
'Golden Torch'
Flower size: 8 cm (3¼ in)
Height: 100 cm (39 in)
Stem: 10–20 cm (4–8 in)

17. Decorative dahlia
'Caramel Antique'
Flower size: 11 cm (4½ in)
Height: 120 cm (47 in)
Stem: 20–30 cm (8–12 in)

18. Waterlily dahlia
'Glorie van Heemstede'
Flower size: 11 cm (4½ in)
Height: 130 cm (51 in)
Stem: 20–30 cm (8–12 in)

19. Laciniated dahlia
'Canary Fubuki'
Flower size: 12 cm (5 in)
Height: 110 cm (43 in)
Stem: 10–30 cm (4–12 in)

20

22   21

23

24

25

26

20. Decorative dahlia

'Ace Summer Sunset'

Flower size: 17 cm (6½ in)
Height: 150 cm (5 ft)
Stem: 20 cm (8 in)

21. Collarette dahlia

'Appleblossom'

Flower size: 10–12 cm (4–5 in)
Height: 130 cm (51 in)
Stem: 10–20 cm (4–8 in)

22. Ball dahlia

'Blyton Softer Gleam'

Flower size: 9–12 cm (3½–5 in)
Height: 100–120 cm (39–47 in)
Stem: 20 cm (8 in)

23. Ball dahlia

'Jowey Nicky'

Flower size: 11 cm (4½ in)
Height: 110 cm (43 in)
Stem: 30 cm (12 in)

24. Semi-cactus dahlia

'Gold Crown'

Flower size: 17 cm (6½ in)
Height: 120 cm (47 in)
Stem: 20–30 cm (8–12 in)

25. Semi-cactus dahlia

'Cabana Banana'

Flower size: 15–17 cm (6– 6½ in)
Height: 100–120 cm (39–47 in)
Stem: 20–30 cm (8–12 in)

26. Decorative dahlia

'Mats'

Flower size: 13 cm (5¼ in)
Height: 80 cm (32 in)
Stem: 80 cm (32 in)

27. Decorative dahlia

'Wittem'

Flower size: 12 cm (5 in)
Height: 60 cm (24 in)
Stem: 10 cm (4 in)

28. Pompom dahlia

'White Aster'

Flower size: 5 cm (2 in)
Height: 130 cm (51 in)
Stem: 15 cm (6 in)

29. Collarette dahlia

'Twyning's White Chocolate'

Flower size: 12 cm (5 in)
Height: 100 cm (39 in)
Stem: 20 cm (8 in)

30. Decorative dahlia

'White Alva's'

Flower size: 25 cm (10 in)
Height: 90 cm (36 in)
Stem: 10–20 cm (4–8 in)

31. Laciniated dahlia

'Tsuki-yori-no-shisha'

Flower size: 16 cm (6¼ in)
Height: 100 cm (39 in)
Stem: 30 cm (12 in)

32. Laciniated dahlia
'Myama Fubuki'
Flower size: 10 cm (4 in)
Height: 120 cm (47 in)
Stem: 20–30 (8–12 in)

33. Ball dahlia
'Petra's Wedding'
Flower size: 7–8 cm (3–3¼ in)
Height: 100 cm (39 in)
Stem: 10–20 cm (4–8 in)

34. Semi-cactus dahlia
'My Love'
Flower size: 11 cm (4½ in)
Height: 120 cm (47 in)
Stem: 20–30 cm (8–12 in)

35. Single-flowered dahlia
'Mignon White'
Flower size: 4 cm (1½ in)
Height: 60 cm (24 in)
Stem: 10 cm (4 in)

36. Semi-cactus dahlia
'Klondike'
Flower size: 20–25 cm (8–10 in)
Height: 120–140 cm (47–55 in)
Stem: 20–30 cm (8–12 in)

37. Waterlily dahlia
'Karma Maarten Zwaan'
Flower size: 11–14 cm
Height: 100 cm (39 in)
Stem: 10–20 cm (4–8 in)

38. Anemone-flowering dahlia
'Platinum Blonde'
Flower size: 12 cm (5 in)
Height: 100 cm (39 in)
Stem: 10–30 cm (4–12 in)

39. Single orchid dahlia (star-shaped)
'Honka White'
Flower size: 14 cm (5½ in)
Height: 120 cm (47 in)
Stem: 20 cm (8 in)

37

38

39

40

41

42

43

40. Laciniated dahlia
'Fleurel'
Flower size: 20 cm (8 in)
Height: 100 cm (39 in)
Stem: 10–20 cm (4–8 in)

41. Pompom dahlia
'Small World'
Flower size: 5 cm (2 in)
Height: 120 cm (47 in)
Stem: 20 cm (8 in)

42. Single-flowered dahlia
'Dahlegria White'
Flower size: 10 cm (4 in)
Height: 55 cm (22 in)
Stem: 20 cm (8 in)

43. Ball dahlia
'Boom Boom White'
Flower size: 12 cm (5 in)
Height: 180 cm (6 ft)
Stem: 30 cm (12 in)

44. Decorative dahlia
'Eveline'
Flower size: 10 cm (4 in)
Height: 120 cm (47 in)
Stem: 20–40 cm (8–16 in)

45. Decorative dahlia
'Shiloh Noelle'
Flower size: 23 cm (9 in)
Height: 140 cm (55 in)
Stem: 30–40 cm (12–16 in)

46. Decorative dahlia
'Arbatax'
Flower size: 10 cm (4 in)
Height: 90 cm (36 in)
Stem: 20 cm (8 in)

47. Peony dahlia
'Bishop of Dover'
Flower size: 9 cm (3½ in)
Height: 120 cm (47 in)
Stem: 10 cm (4 in)

48. Peony dahlia
'Bishop of Leicester'
Flower size: 10 cm (4 in)
Height: 100 cm (39 in)
Stem: 10–30 cm (4–12 in)

49. Decorative dahlia
'Bonesta'
Flower size: 10 cm (4 in)
Height: 100 cm (39 in)
Stem: 20–30 cm (8–12 in)

50. Ball dahlia
'Janick's Symphony'
Flower size: 10 cm (4 in)
Height: 100 cm (39 in)
Stem: 20–30 cm (8–12 in)

51. Decorative dahlia
'Prince Valiant'
Flower size: 14 cm (5½ in)
Height: 130 cm (51 in)
Stem: 10–15 cm (4–6 in)

52. Single orchid dahlia (star-shaped)
'Destiny's Teachers'
Flower size: 9 cm (3½ in)
Height: 100 cm (39 in)
Stem: 20–30 cm (8–12 in)

53. Semi-cactus dahlia
'Mick's Peppermint'
Flower size: 20 cm (8 in)
Height: 130–140 cm (51–55 in)
Stem: 10 cm (4 in)

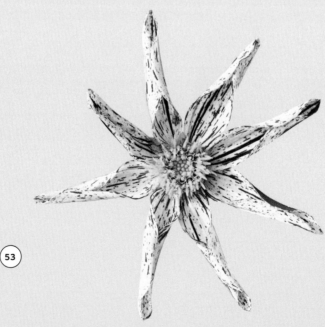

51

52

53

54. Decorative dahlia
'Little Tiger'
Flower size: 10 cm (4 in)
Height: 50 cm (20 in)
Stem: 10 cm (4 in)

55. Decorative dahlia
'Santa Claus'
Flower size: 12 cm (5 in)
Height: 100–110 cm (39–43 in)
Stem: 10–30 cm (4–12 in)

56. Decorative dahlia
'Rainbow Silence'
Flower size: 13 cm (5¼ in)
Height: 100–120 cm (39–47 in)
Stem: 10–15 cm (4–6 in)

54
55
56
57
58
59

57. Collarette dahlia

'Pooh'

Flower size: 10 cm (4 in)
Height: 110 cm (43 in)
Stem: 10–20 cm (4–8 in)

58. Single orchid dahlia (star-shaped)

'Windmill'

Flower size: 10–15 cm (4–6 in)
Height: 100 cm (39 in)
Stem: 10–30 cm (4–12 in)

59. Anemone-flowering dahlia

'Bon Odori'

Flower size: 10 cm (4 in)
Height: 110 cm (43 in)
Stem: 20 cm (8 in)

60. Ball dahlia
'Salsa'
Flower size: 7 cm (3 in)
Height: 125 cm (4 ft)
Stem: 20–25 cm (8–10 in)

61. Decorative dahlia
'Red Cap'
Flower size: 10 cm (4 in)
Height: 130 cm (51 in)
Stem: 30 cm (12 in)

62. Decorative dahlia
'Gallery Singer'
Flower size: 8 cm (3¼ in)
Height: 50 cm (20 in)
Stem: 10–20 cm (4–8 in)

63. Ball dahlia
'Red Symphony'
Flower size: 10 cm (4 in)
Height: 130 cm (51 in)
Stem: 20 cm (8 in)

64. Cactus dahlia
'Forrestal'
Flower size: 16 cm (6¼ in)
Height: 110–140 cm (43–55 in)
Stem: 30–40 cm (12–16 in)

65. Decorative dahlia
'Red Labyrinth'
Flower size: 23 cm (9 in)
Height: 90–100 cm (36–39 in)
Stem: 10–30 cm (4–12 in)

66
67
68
69

66. Collarette dahlia
'Mary Evelyn'
Flower size: 8–10 cm (3¼–4 in)
Height: 70–90 cm (27–36 in)
Stem: 15–25 cm (6–10 in)

67. Decorative dahlia
'Contraste'
Flower size: 20 cm (8 in)
Height: 90 cm (36 in)
Stem: 20 cm (8 in)

68. Decorative dahlia
'Checkers'
Flower size: 9 cm (3½ in)
Height: 120 cm (47 in)
Stem: 10–25 cm (4–10 in)

69. Single orchid dahlia (star-shaped)
'Honka Rood'
Flower size: 13 cm (5¼ in)
Height: 130 cm (51 in)
Stem: 10–20 cm (4–8 in)

70. Decorative dahlia
'Baccara'
Flower size: 11 cm (4½ in)
Height: 100 cm (39 in)
Stem: 10 cm (4 in)

71. Ball dahlia
'Cornel'
Flower size: 9 cm (3½ in)
Height: 150 cm (5 ft)
Stem: 30 cm (12 in)

72. Pompom dahlia
'Ivanetti'
Flower size: 7–8 cm (3–3¼ in)
Height: 150 cm (5 ft)
Stem: 10–30 cm (4–12 in)

73. Decorative dahlia
'Zorro'
Flower size: 20–25 cm (8–10 in)
Height: 100–130 cm (39–51 in)
Stem: 20–40 cm (8–16 in)

74. Laciniated dahlia
'Dark Fubuki'
Flower size: 12 cm (5 in)
Height: 120 cm (47 in)
Stem: 20 cm (8 in)

70
71
72
73
74

75 76 77

75. Single orchid dahlia (star-shaped)
'Veronne's Obsidian'
Flower size: 11 cm (4½ in)
Height: 110 cm (43 in)
Stem: 11 cm (4½ in)

76. Decorative dahlia
'Dark Spirit'
Flower size: 7 cm (3 in)
Height: 100–120 cm (39–47 in)
Stem: 10–20 cm (4–8 in)

77. Pompom dahlia
'Jowey Mirella'
Flower size: 8 cm (3¼ in)
Height: 110 cm (43 in)
Stem: 10–30 cm (4–12 in)

78. Decorative dahlia
'Hans Auinger'
Flower size: 15 cm (6 in)
Height: 110 cm (43 in)
Stem: 30 cm (12 in)

79. Waterlily dahlia
'Rawhide'
Flower size: 10 cm (4 in)
Height: 100–130 cm (4–10 in)
Stem: 5–20 cm (2–8 in)

80. Anemone-flowering dahlia
'Totally Tangerine'
Flower size: 8–10 cm (3¼–4 in)
Height: 60–100 cm (24–39 in)
Stem: 10 cm (4 in)

81. Pompom dahlia
'Cornel Brons'
Flower size: 8 cm (3¼ in)
Height: 90–120 cm (36–47 in)
Stem: 10–20 cm (4–8 in)

82. Decorative dahlia
'Safe Shot'
Flower size: 8 cm (3¼ in)
Height: 100 cm (39 in)
Stem: 20 cm (8 in)

83. Decorative dahlia
'Sugar Cane'
Flower size: 10–15 cm (4–6 in)
Height: 130 cm (51 in)
Stem: 10–20 cm (4–8 in)

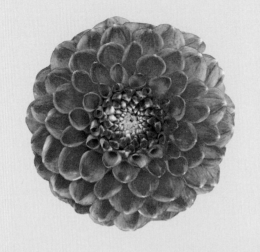

84. Ball dahlia
'Snoho Doris'
Flower size: 9–12 cm (3½–5 in)
Height: 140 cm (55 in)
Stem: 30 cm (12 in)

85. Pompom dahlia
'Nuland's Josephine'
Flower size: 5 cm (2 in)
Height: 150 cm (5 ft)
Stem: 10 cm (4 in)

86. Pompom dahlia
'Bantling'
Flower size: 8–9 cm (3¼–3½ in)
Height: 120 cm (47 in)
Stem: 10–15 cm (4–6 in)

87. Anemone-flowering dahlia
'Bouton Pêche'
Flower size: 9 cm (3½ in)
Height: 110 cm (43 in)
Stem: 10–20 cm (4–8 in)

88. Decorative dahlia
'Pacific View'
Flower size: 20 cm (8 in)
Height: 110 cm (43 in)
Stem: 20 cm (8 in)

89. Decorative dahlia
'Parkland Glory'
Flower size: 15 cm (6 in)
Height: 110 cm (43 in)
Stem: 20–30 cm (8–12 in)

84
85
86
87
88
89

90

91

92

93

90. Decorative dahlia
'Great Hercules'
Flower size: 22 cm (8½ in)
Height: 90 cm (36 in)
Stem: 30 cm (12 in)

91. Decorative dahlia
'Orange Pekoe'
Flower size: 13 cm (5¼ in)
Height: 120 cm (47 in)
Stem: 10–20 cm (4–8 in)

92. Pompom dahlia
'Sylvia'
Flower size: 11 cm (4½ in)
Height: 100 cm (39 in)
Stem: 20 cm (8 in)

93. Semi-cactus dahlia
'Orange Pygmy'
Flower size: 10 cm (4 in)
Height: 55 cm (22 in)
Stem: 10 cm (4 in)

94

95

96

94. Decorative dahlia
'Babylon Brons'
Flower size: 20–25 cm (8–10 in)
Height: 100–120 cm (39–47 in)
Stem: 10–30 cm (4–12 in)

95. Decorative dahlia
'Noordwijks Glorie'
Flower size: 12 cm (5 in)
Height: 120 cm (47 in)
Stem: 20–40 cm (8–16 in)

96. Decorative dahlia
'Nicholas'
Flower size: 12–15 cm (5–6 in)
Height: 100–110 cm (39–43 in)
Stem: 5–10 cm (2–4 in)

97. Laciniated dahlia
'Hapet Perfekt'
Flower size: 15–20 cm (6–8 in)
Height: 120 cm (47 in)
Stem: 20–40 cm (8–16 in)

98. Ball dahlia
'Jowey Paula'
Flower size: 8–10 cm (3¼–4 in)
Height: 90 cm (36 in)
Stem: 40 cm (16 in)

99. Pompom dahlia
'Jowey Linda'
Flower size: 10 cm (4 in)
Height: 130 cm (51 in)
Stem: 30 cm (12 in)

100. Laciniated dahlia
'Myrtle's Folly'
Flower size: 18 cm (7 in)
Height: 120 cm (47 in)
Stem: 30 cm (12 in)

101. Decorative dahlia
'Fairway Spur'
Flower size: 20–23 cm (8–9 in)
Height: 100 cm (39 in)
Stem: 30–35 cm (12–15 in)

102. Ball dahlia
'Hapet Salmon'
Flower size: 7–10 cm (3–4 in)
Height: 120 cm (47 in)
Stem: 10–20 cm (4–8 in)

103. Single-flowered dahlia
'HS First Love'
Flower size: 9 cm (3½ in)
Height: 70 cm (27 in)
Stem: 30 cm (12 in)

104. Anemone-flowering dahlia
'Fata Morgana'
Flower size: 10 cm (4 in)
Height: 110 cm (43 in)
Stem: 10–20 cm (4–8 in)

105. Decorative dahlia
'Striped Duet'
Flower size: 17 cm (6½ in)
Height: 80 cm (32 in)
Stem: 30 cm (12 in)

106. Ball dahlia
'Copperboy'
Flower size: 10 cm (4 in)
Height: 90 cm (36 in)
Stem: 20–30 cm (8–12 in)

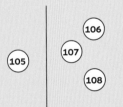

107. Pompom dahlia
'Brown Sugar'
Flower size: 10 cm (4 in)
Height: 120 cm (47 in)
Stem: 20–50 cm (8–20 in)

108. Decorative dahlia
'Daisy Duke'
Flower size: 8 cm (3¼ in)
Height: 100–120 cm (39–47 in)
Stem: 20–30 cm (8–12 in)

109. Waterlily dahlia
'Twilight Time'
Flower size: 10–15 cm (4–6 in)
Height: 100–120 cm (39–47 in)
Stem: 10 cm (4 in)

110. Pompom dahlia
'Genova'
Flower size: 6 cm (2½ in)
Height: 110 cm (43 in)
Stem: 10–20 cm (4–8 in)

111. Waterlily dahlia
'Blue Wish'
Flower size:
11 cm (4½ in)
Height: 80–100 cm
(32–39 in)
Stem: 30 cm (12 in)

112. Decorative dahlia
'Bitsy'
Flower size: 10 cm (4 in)
Height: 80 cm (32 in)
Stem: 10 cm (4 in)

113. Decorative dahlia
'Who Me?'
Flower size: 20 cm (8 in)
Height: 150 cm (5 ft)
Stem: 30–40 cm (12–16 in)

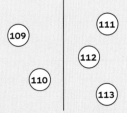

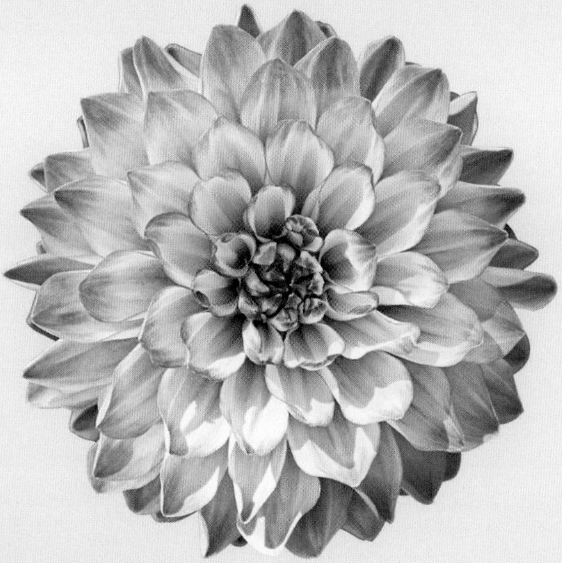

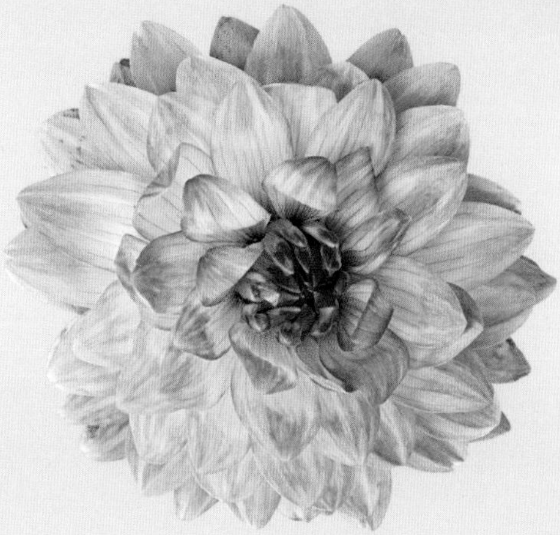

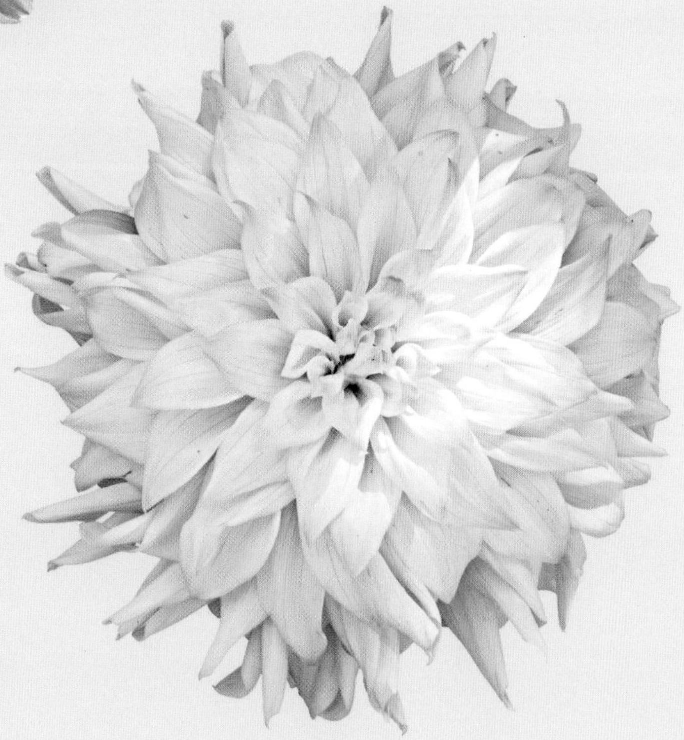

114. Laciniated dahlia
'Table Dancer'
Flower size: 12 cm (5 in)
Height: 100 cm (39 in)
Stem: 5 cm (2 in)

115. Decorative dahlia
'Blue Bell'
Flower size: 11 cm (4½ in)
Height: 80 cm (32 in)
Stem: 20 cm (8 in)

116. Decorative dahlia
'Edinburgh'
Flower size: 9 cm (3½ in)
Height: 150 cm (5 ft)
Stem: 10 cm (4 in)

(114)   (117)
　(115)
(116)　　(118)

117. Decorative dahlia
'Pink Pettycoat'
Flower size: 15 cm (6 in)
Height: 130 cm (51 in)
Stem: 20–30 cm (8–12 in)

118. Waterlily dahlia
'Saint Martin'
Flower size: 10 cm (4 in)
Height: 110 cm (43 in)
Stem: 10–20 cm (4–8 in)

119. Decorative dahlia
'Clearview Debby'

Flower size: 12 cm (5 in)
Height: 110 cm (43 in)
Stem: 20–40 cm (8–16 in)

120. Decorative dahlia
'Bahama Mama'

Flower size: 10 cm (4 in)
Height: 130 cm (51 in)
Stem: 10 cm (4 in)

121. Laciniated dahlia
'Clair Obscur'

Flower size: 15 cm (6 in)
Height: 90 cm (36 in)
Stem: 30–40 cm (12–16 in)

122. Decorative dahlia
'Bristol Stripe'

Flower size: 22 cm (8½ in)
Height: 120 cm (47 in)
Stem: 10–20 cm (4–8 in)

123. Anemone-flowering dahlia
'Dad's Favourite'

Flower size: 13 cm (5¼ in)
Height: 90 cm (36 in)
Stem: 20–30 cm (8–12 in)

124. Single-flowered dahlia
'Delta'

Flower size: 13 cm (5¼ in)
Height: 150–200 cm (5–7 ft)
Stem: 20 cm (8 in)

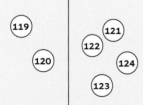

125. Pompom dahlia
'Robann Royal'
Flower size: 9 cm (3½ in)
Height: 90 cm (36 in)
Stem: 20 cm (8 in)

126. Decorative dahlia
'Crème de Cassis'
Flower size: 9 cm (3½ in)
Height: 60–90 cm (24–36 in)
Stem: 10 cm (4 in)

127. Pompom dahlia
'Frank Holmes'
Flower size: 4–5 cm (1½–2 in)
Height: 40 cm (16 in)
Stem: 5 cm (2 in)

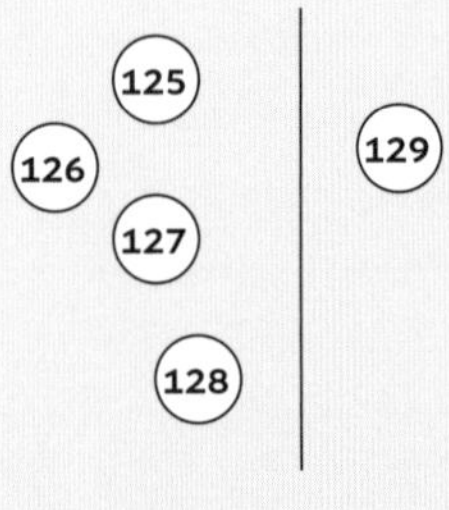

125
126
127
128

129

128. Single orchid dahlia (star-shaped)
'Honka Pink'
Flower size: 10 cm (4 in)
Height: 120 cm (47 in)
Stem: 20 cm (8 in)

129. Semi-cactus dahlia
'American Dream'
Flower size: 15 cm (6 in)
Height: 120 cm (47 in)
Stem: 10–20 cm (4–8 in)

130. Decorative dahlia
'Patches'

Flower size: 16 cm (6¼ in)
Height: 110 cm (43 in)
Stem: 20 cm (8 in)

131. Cactus dahlia
'Hy Trio'

Flower size: 15 cm (6 in)
Height: 100–120 cm
(39–47 in)
Stem: 20–30 cm (8–12 in)

132. Decorative dahlia
'Romantica'

Flower size: 10 cm (4 in)
Height: 90 cm (36 in)
Stem: 20–30 cm (8–12 in)

133. Decorative dahlia
'Purple Pearl'

Flower size: 15 cm (6 in)
Height: 150 cm (5 ft)
Stem: 20 cm (8 in)

134. Decorative dahlia
'Thomas Edison'

Flower size: 15 cm (6 in)
Height: 120 cm (47 in)
Stem: 20 cm (8 in)

135. Ball dahlia
'Purple Fox'

Flower size: 8 cm (3¼ in)
Height: 90 cm (36 in)
Stem: 10–20 cm (4–8 in)

136. Decorative dahlia
'Smiling Don'

Flower size: 8 cm (3¼ in)
Height: 100 cm (39 in)
Stem: 20 cm (8 in)

137. Decorative dahlia
'Otto's Thrill'
Flower size: 22 cm (8½ in)
Height: 110 cm (43 in)
Stem: 20–30 cm (8–12 in)

138. Decorative dahlia
'Pink Suffusion'
Flower size: 10 cm (4 in)
Height: 90 cm (36 in)
Stem: 10 cm (4 in)

139. Decorative dahlia
'Molly Raven'
Flower size: 11 cm (4½ in)
Height: 120 cm (47 in)
Stem: 10–20 cm (4–8 in)

140. Pompom dahlia
'Little Robert'
Flower size: 4–5 cm (1½–2 in)
Height: 100 cm (39 in)
Stem: 10–22 cm (4–8½ in)

141. Decorative dahlia
'Melody Lizza'
Flower size: 10–12 cm (4–5 in)
Height: 50 cm (20 in)
Stem: 10 cm (4 in)

142

144

145

143

146

142. Decorative dahlia
'Purple Taiheijo'
Flower size: 23 cm (9 in)
Height: 110 cm (43 in)
Stem: 10–20 cm (4–8 in)

143. Decorative dahlia
'Mero Star'
Flower size: 17 cm (6½ in)
Height: 110 cm (43 in)
Stem: 10 cm (4 in)

144. Waterlily dahlia
'Priceless Pink'
Flower size: 7 cm (3 in)
Height: 50 cm (20 in)
Stem: 10 cm (4 in)

145. Decorative dahlia
'Purple Ice'
Flower size: 10–12 cm (4–5 in)
Height: 130 cm (51 in)
Stem: 20–30 cm (8–12 in)

146. Collarette dahlia
'Skyfall'
Flower size: 10 cm (4 in)
Height: 120 cm (47 in)
Stem: 10–30 cm (4–12 in)

147

148

149

150

147. Decorative dahlia
'Almand's Joy'
Flower size: 23 cm (9 in)
Height: 100 cm (39 in)
Stem: 20–30 cm (8–12 in)

148. Decorative dahlia
'Chilson's Pride'
Flower size: 10 cm (4 in)
Height: 120–140 cm
Stem: 20 cm (8 in)

149. Decorative dahlia
'Strawberry Cream'
Flower size: 7 cm (3 in)
Height: 80–100 cm (32–39 in)
Stem: 10–20 cm (4–8 in)

150. Decorative dahlia
'Ariko 51-16'
Flower size: 12 cm (5 in)
Height: 110 cm (43 in)
Stem: 20–40 cm (8–16 in)

151. Ball dahlia
'Wizard of Oz'
Flower size: 7–9 cm (3–3½ in)
Height: 130 cm (51 in)
Stem: 35 cm (15 in)

152. Ball dahlia
'Snoho Sonia'
Flower size: 10–20 cm (4–8 in)
Height: 90 cm (36 in)
Stem: 30 cm (12 in)

153. Pompom dahlia
'Maiike'
Flower size: 4 cm (1½ in)
Height: 80–90 cm (32–36 in)
Stem: 10 cm (4 in)

151
152
155
153
156
154

154. Ball dahlia
'Willowfield Matthews'
Flower size: 7 cm (3 in)
Height: 170 cm (5½ ft)
Stem: 30 cm (12 in)

155. Decorative dahlia
'Labyrinth Twotone'
Flower size: 20 cm (8 in)
Height: 110 cm (43 in)
Stem: 10–20 cm (4–8 in)

156. Decorative dahlia
'Sweet Love'
Flower size: 10 cm (4 in)
Height: 110 cm (43 in)
Stem: 20–40 cm (8–16 in)

157. Decorative dahlia
'Fuzzy Wuzzy'
Flower size: 9 cm (3½ in)
Height: 100 cm (39 in)
Stem: 5–10 cm (2–4 in)

158. Peony dahlia
'Fascination'
Flower size: 13 cm (5¼ in)
Height: 100–110 cm (39–43 in)
Stem: 20 cm (8 in)

159. Waterlily dahlia
'Berner Oberland'
Flower size: 14 cm (5½ in)
Height: 120 cm (47 in)
Stem: 20–40 cm (8–16 in)

160. Decorative dahlia
'Lavender Perfection'
Flower size: 20 cm (8 in)
Height: 160 cm (5¼ ft)
Stem: 30–50 cm (12–20 in)

161. Decorative dahlia
'Bacardi'
Flower size: 13 cm (5¼ in)
Height: 90 cm (36 in)
Stem: 10–30 cm (4–12 in)

162. Decorative dahlia
'Westerton Ella Grace'
Flower size: 9 cm (3½ in)
Height: 140 cm (55 in)
Stem: 10–20 cm (4–8 in)

163. Decorative dahlia
'Colorado Classic'
Flower size: 14 cm (5½ in)
Height: 130 cm (51 in)
Stem: 20 cm (8 in)

164. Decorative dahlia
'Striped Emory Paul'
Flower size: 28–30 cm (11–12 in)
Height: 120 cm (47 in)
Stem: 40 cm (16 in)

165. Decorative dahlia
'Kiev'
Flower size: 20 cm (8 in)
Height: 80–90 cm (32–36 in)
Stem: 10 cm (4 in)

166. Pompom dahlia
'Jowey Winnie'
Flower size: 9– 11 cm
(4½ in)
Height: 100–120 cm
(39–47 in)
Stem: 20 cm (8 in)

167. Decorative dahlia
'Frost Nip'
Flower size: 20 cm (8 in)
Height: 120 cm (47 in)
Stem: 10 cm (4 in)

168. Decorative dahlia
'Café au Lait Royal'
Flower size: 25 cm (10 in)
Height: 110 cm (43 in)
Stem: 10 cm (4 in)

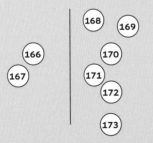

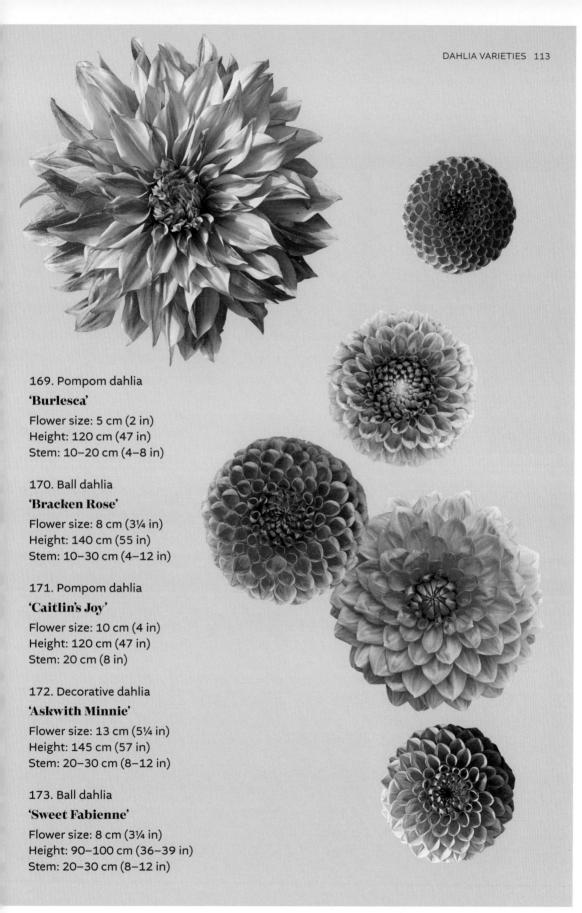

169. Pompom dahlia
'Burlesca'
Flower size: 5 cm (2 in)
Height: 120 cm (47 in)
Stem: 10–20 cm (4–8 in)

170. Ball dahlia
'Bracken Rose'
Flower size: 8 cm (3¼ in)
Height: 140 cm (55 in)
Stem: 10–30 cm (4–12 in)

171. Pompom dahlia
'Caitlin's Joy'
Flower size: 10 cm (4 in)
Height: 120 cm (47 in)
Stem: 20 cm (8 in)

172. Decorative dahlia
'Askwith Minnie'
Flower size: 13 cm (5¼ in)
Height: 145 cm (57 in)
Stem: 20–30 cm (8–12 in)

173. Ball dahlia
'Sweet Fabienne'
Flower size: 8 cm (3¼ in)
Height: 90–100 cm (36–39 in)
Stem: 20–30 cm (8–12 in)

174. Decorative dahlia
'Berliner Kleene'
Flower size: 10 cm (4 in)
Height: 50 cm (20 in)
Stem: 5–10 cm (2–4 in)

175. Decorative dahlia
'Feline Yvonne'
Flower size: 15 cm (6 in)
Height: 120 cm (47 in)
Stem: 20–40 cm (8–16 in)

176. Semi-cactus dahlia
'Samourai'
Flower size: 15 cm (6 in)
Height: 70 cm (27 in)
Stem: 20–30 cm (8–12 in)

177. Ball dahlia
'Babette'
Flower size: 10 cm (4 in)
Height: 100 cm (39 in)
Stem: 10–20 cm (4–8 in)

178. Decorative dahlia
'Heat Wave'
Flower size: 13 cm (5¼ in)
Height: 110 cm (43 in)
Stem: 20 cm (8 in)

179. Waterlily dahlia
'Christine'
Flower size: 12 cm (5 in)
Height: 80 cm (32 in)
Stem: 20 cm (8 in)

180. Decorative dahlia
'American Dawn'
Flower size: 14 cm (5½ in)
Height: 100 cm (39 in)
Stem: 30 cm (12 in)

181. Decorative dahlia
'Perch Hill'
Flower size: 10 cm (4 in)
Height: 140 cm (55 in)
Stem: 20 cm (8 in)

182. Decorative dahlia
'All That Jazz'
Flower size: 13 cm (5¼ in)
Height: 120 cm (47 in)
Stem: 20–35 cm (8–15 in)

183

184

185

186

183. Decorative dahlia
'Labyrinth'
Flower size: 15 cm (6 in)
Height: 100 cm (39 in)
Stem: 10–30 cm (4–12 in)

184. Decorative dahlia
'Holland Festival'
Flower size: 20 cm (8 in)
Height: 120 cm (47 in)
Stem: 20–40 cm (8–16 in)

185. Pompom dahlia
'Linda's Baby'
Flower size: 9–10 cm (3½–4 in)
Height: 90 cm (36 in)
Stem: 20–30 cm (8–12 in)

186. Ball dahlia
'L.A.T.E'
Flower size: 8 cm (3¼ in)
Height: 120–150 cm (3½–5 ft)
Stem: 30 cm (12 in)

187. Ball dahlia
'Sefton Silvertop'
Flower size: 10 cm (4 in)
Height: 140 cm (55 in)
Stem: 20 cm (8 in)

188. Decorative dahlia
'Café au Lait Twist'
Flower size: 20 cm (8 in)
Height: 110 cm (43 in)
Stem: 10–20 cm (4–8 in)

189. Decorative dahlia
'Pink Skin'
Flower size: 12 cm (5 in)
Height: 130 cm (51 in)
Stem: 30 cm (12 in)

190. Decorative dahlia
'Karma Amanda'
Flower size: 15 cm (6 in)
Height: 80 cm (32 in)
Stem: 5–10 cm (2–4 in)

191. Decorative dahlia
'Babylon Lilac'
Flower size: 20 cm (8 in)
Height: 100–120 cm
(39–47 in)
Stem: 20–40 cm (8–16 in)

192. Single-flowered dahlia
'Topmix Pink'
Flower size: 6 cm (2½ in)
Height: 50 cm (20 in)
Stem: 10 cm (4 in)

193. Laciniated dahlia
'Pinelands Princess'
Flower size: 14 cm (5½ in)
Height: 120 cm (47 in)
Stem: 10–20 cm (4–8 in)

194. Anemone-flowering dahlia
'Mambo'
Flower size: 13 cm (5¼ in)
Height: 120 cm (47 in)
Stem: 40 cm (16 in)

195. Laciniated dahlia
'Kogane Fubuki'
Flower size: 11 cm (4½ in)
Height: 80–90 cm (32–36 in)
Stem: 20 cm (8 in)

192
193
196
197
194
195

196. Cactus dahlia
'Lindsay Michelle'
Flower size: 15 cm (6 in)
Height: 100 cm (39 in)
Stem: 20 cm (8 in)

197. Decorative dahlia
'Armateras'
Flower size: 15 cm (6 in)
Height: 100 cm (39 in)
Stem: 25 cm (10 in)

198. Decorative dahlia
'Temple of Beauty'
Flower size: 20 cm (8 in)
Height: 110 cm (43 in)
Stem: 20 cm (8 in)

199. Decorative dahlia
'Trustfull'
Flower size: 10 cm (4 in)
Height: 60 cm (24 in)
Stem: 10–12 cm (4–5 in)

200. Decorative dahlia
'Hawaii'
Flower size: 9–10 cm (3½–4 in)
Height: 120 cm (47 in)
Stem: 20 cm (8 in)

201. Anemone-flowering dahlia
'Life Style'
Flower size: 10 cm (4 in)
Height: 80 cm (32 in)
Stem: 10–20 cm (4–8 in)

202. Decorative dahlia
'Café au Lait'
Flower size: 22 cm (8½ in)
Height: 130 cm (51 in)
Stem: 10–30 cm (4–12 in)

203. Decorative dahlia
'Break Out'
Flower size: 16 cm (6¼ in)
Height: 110 cm (43 in)
Stem: 10–20 cm (4–8 in)

204. Decorative dahlia
'Sweet Nathalie'
Flower size: 13 cm (5¼ in)
Height: 100 cm (39 in)
Stem: 20 cm (8 in)

205. Semi-cactus dahlia
'Henriette'
Flower size: 10 cm (4 in)
Height: 100–110 cm
(39–43 in)
Stem: 40 cm (16 in)

206. Decorative dahlia
'Happy Butterfly'
Flower size: 15 cm (6 in)
Height: 130 cm (51 in)
Stem: 20–30 cm (8–12 in)

207. Decorative dahlia
'Zingaro'
Flower size: 10 cm (4 in)
Height: 60 cm (24 in)
Stem: 20 cm (8 in)

208. Waterlily dahlia
'Crème de Cognac'
Flower size: 10 cm (4 in)
Height: 75 cm (30 in)
Stem: 20 cm (8 in)

209. Ball dahlia
'Wine Eyed Jill'
Flower size: 8 cm (3¼ in)
Height: 90–130 cm (36 in–4 ft)
Stem: 20–35 cm (12–20 in)

210. Decorative dahlia
'Hapet Pastell'
Flower size: 15 cm (6 in)
Height: 140 cm (55 in)
Stem: 10–20 cm (4–8 in)

211. Ball dahlia
'Valley Tawny'
Flower size: 8 cm (3¼ in)
Height: 100–120 cm (39–47 in)
Stem: 15 cm (6 in)

212. Decorative dahlia
'Peaches n'Cream'
Flower size: 11 cm (4½ in)
Height: 140 cm (55 in)
Stem: 20 cm (8 in)

213. Decorative dahlia
'Maya'
Flower size: 10–13 cm (4–5¼ in)
Height: 70 cm (27 in)
Stem: 10–20 cm (4–8 in)

216. Semi-cactus dahlia
'Preference'
Flower size: 12 cm (5 in)
Height: 90 cm (36 in)
Stem: 26–35 cm (10¼–15 in)

214. Decorative dahlia
'Tyrell'
Flower size: 20 cm (8 in)
Height: 100 cm (39 in)
Stem: 20 cm (8 in)

217. Ball dahlia
'Hamari Rose'
Flower size: 8–10 cm (3¼–4 in)
Height: 90–130 cm (36–51 in)
Stem: 20 cm (8 in)

215. Decorative dahlia
'Valley Porcupine'
Flower size: 9 cm (3½ in)
Height: 80 cm (32 in)
Stem: 5 cm (2 in)

218. Decorative dahlia
'Penhill Watermelon'
Flower size: 20–30 cm (8–12 in)
Height: 120–170 cm (47–67 in)
Stem: 30–40 cm (12–16 in)

(214)
(215)
(216)
(217)
(218)

219. Decorative dahlia

'Pasadoble Dancer'

Flower size: 22 cm (8½ in)
Height: 80 cm (32 in)
Stem: 10–30 cm (4–12 in)

220. Laciniated dahlia

'Apricot Star'

Flower size: 15–17 cm (6– 6½ in)
Height: 100–120 cm (39–47 in)
Stem: 20 cm (8 in)

221. Collarette dahlia

'Teesbrook Audrey'

Flower size: 10 cm (4 in)
Height: 130 cm (51 in)
Stem: 20–30 cm (8–12 in)

222. Laciniated dahlia

'Omega'

Flower size: 17 cm (6½ in)
Height: 90–100 cm (36–39 in)
Stem: 20 cm (8 in)

Dahlia inspiration

There's so much pleasure to be had with dahlias. Planning a flower bed and finding accompanying plants for them is wonderful, as is making beautiful bouquets and table settings with dahlias. You can even dry your dahlias so you can enjoy them all year round!

ULRIKA'S DAHLIAS GROWING IN RAISED BEDS MADE OF PLASTERED
LECA BLOCKS. THE DAHLIAS ARE IN A WARM POSITION HERE AND
IT'S HARDER FOR SLUGS AND SNAILS TO GET TO THEM.

Dahlias in the flower bed

For dahlia enthusiasts like us there's hardly anything that compares to designing dahlia beds, as every year there are endless new possibilities when you come to renew the feel of your beds and what they express. Apart from planning different colour combinations, it's important to keep your eye on heights. If you have a flower bed along a wall or fence, the tallest dahlias should be positioned at the back and the shortest ones at the front.

Colour upon colour

Beds of flowers of the same colour can be very beautiful. Mix dahlias of different heights or with flowers of different shapes and sizes. You can also mix dahlias of the same colour from the different groups, making for dahlia magic. Various shades of red will signal romance and drama, and can be very effective.

Pastels
Pastel colours are muted versions of yellow, pink, peach and lilac that create softness and attractive hues in the bed.

Yellow
A lot of people avoid yellow, but mixing different dahlia varieties in many shades of yellow can make for a truly eye-catching display.

Coral
Coral and orange are strong colours that can be toned down by creamier-coloured dahlias. These contrasts create exciting encounters between the varieties. Mixing different dahlia varieties in a host of colours and shapes will give the beholder a wonderful feeling. And feel free to mix multicoloured varieties to achieve a lovely effect.

'WINE EYED JILL' DELIVERS LOVELY LITTLE LONG-STEMMED BALLS THROUGHOUT THE SEASON. INITIALLY THE FLOWERS WILL INCLUDE A LOT OF CERISE, WHICH THEN TRANSITIONS TO PALE PINK AND YELLOW. AT THE END OF THE SEASON THE FLOWERS WILL BE ALMOST COMPLETELY YELLOW.

'AMERICAN DAWN', 'WINE EYED JILL', 'LINDA'S BABY' AND 'SHILOH NOELLE', ALL WITH LONG STEMS AND GOOD FOR CUT FLOWERS.

'LINDA'S BABY' AND 'WINE EYED JILL'

'PENHILL WATERMELON'

'BROWN SUGAR'

'BURLESCA'

'WIZARD OF OZ', 'CORNEL', 'WESTERTON ELLA GRACE',
'SEFTON SILVERTOP' AND 'BABYLON BRONZE'.

Companion planting

You can, of course, just use dahlias in your flower beds but adding other plants creates another dimension.

Crown dill, *Anethum graveolens*

Perhaps not an obvious accompaniment to dahlias, but crown dill's yellow flowers are beautiful. It goes well with 'Wine Eyed Jill', which is tinged with yellow for a few weeks of the season, as well as with coral-coloured varieties.

GROWING: Sow indoors in the spring.

Purpletop vervain, *Verbena bonariensis*

This annual purpletop vervain is a summer favourite that flowers for as long as dahlias. It is tall and easy to grow, and its little flowers against dahlias' much bigger ones create great contrasts.

GROWING: Sow in early spring or in the autumn. At nurseries you can also find garden-ready plants. If you're overwintering your dahlias anyway, you can dig up the purpletop vervain plants and store them in pots in the same frost-free location. Give them a little water a few times during the winter. Once you've grown purpletop vervain small plants will tend to appear at the same location in the spring – or they do in my home in Sweden – when the seeds released by the purpletop vervain in the summer and autumn have started to sprout.

CROWN DILL IS ATTRACTIVE PAIRED WITH
PALE-PINK AND YELLOW DAHLIAS, AND THERE
WILL BE A LOVELY SCENT WHEN YOU WALK PAST.

'EDINBURGH' ON THE VERGE OF BLOSSOMING.

WHITE AND LILAC SWEET PEAS ARE LOVELY
TOGETHER WITH 'SHILOH NOELLE' AND 'EVELINE'.

Sunflower, *Helianthus annuus*

'Ruby Eclipse' is the name of this sunflower, whose rusty shades will compete for attention with the tall dahlias in the bed. It grows to approximately 180 cm (6 ft) in height and flowers profusely.

GROWING: Sow them straight into the soil in the growing site, but if you've already planted the dahlias out, make sure the location for the sunflower seeds isn't too shady.

Zinnia, *Zinnia*

New varieties of zinnia have emerged in recent years. They last a long time in both flower beds and bouquets and are a great companion flower for the front of the dahlia bed. Choose between apricot, pink, lime, yellow, red and orange, or select effective varieties featuring speckles or stripes.

GROWING: Start off indoors in spring and plant out when the risk of frost has passed. Harden the plants off beforehand by acclimatizing them to sunlight for a few hours a day. Zinnias can also be sown straight into the soil in the growing site, but they will then bloom later.

PURPLETOP VERVAIN

PHLOX DRUMMONDII

BLACK-EYED SUSAN 'SAHARA'

SUNFLOWER 'RUBY ECLIPSE'

A HOST OF DAHLIAS IN MALMÖ'S CASTLE GARDEN.

Black-eyed Susan, *Rudbeckia hirta var. pulcherrima*

Black-eyed Susan – in particular the variety 'Sahara' – has become a common sight in bouquets, often coupled with 'Café au Lait'. The unique colour scale with its rusty shades of yellow, caramel pink and dark red creates extraordinary contrasts in the dahlia bed. 'Sahara' grows to a height of approximately 60 cm (24 in).

GROWING: Start off indoors in the spring in sowing soil and plant out when the risk of frost has passed. Harden the plants off beforehand by acclimatizing them to sunlight for a few hours a day.

Phlox drummondii, *Phlox drummondii*

Another annual that's often seen with dahlias is *Phlox drummondii*, particularly lovely when paired with 'Cherry Caramel' and 'Blushing Bride', which are fast disappearing from the seed companies' stock; you'll need to act fast if you want to try this combination. The height of 'Blushing Bride' is approximately 50 cm (20 in), and that of 'Cherry Caramel' is 10 cm (4 in) less. Both are perfect for cut flowers.

GROWING: Start off indoors in spring in sowing soil and plant out when the risk of frost has passed. Harden the plants off beforehand by acclimatizing them to sunlight for a few hours a day.

Dahlias as cut flowers

Dahlias are fantastic in bouquets, and if you look after the cut flowers they will last for five days or more in a vase. Ball dahlias keep longer than large, shaggy dinner-plate dahlias. Stem length varies from dahlia to dahlia and those with the longest stems go best with bouquets, whilst those with short stems can be used in small vases or water baths.

Seven tips to help dahlias keep longer in vases

1. Harvest the flowers in good time. If they're to be used the same day they should just have opened up, but if you're making a bouquet for the following day it's better if the flowers are just on the verge of opening. Dahlia buds find it hard to open up in vases.

2. Pick the dahlias in the morning or the evening when it's cool, as that's when they hold the most sap.

3. Make slanting cuts with a clean flower knife and have a clean bucket of fresh water at hand, where you can place the flowers as soon as you've picked them.

4. Change the water every other day and wash out the vase with washing-up liquid.

5. Cut fresh flowers every other day.

6. Don't position the vase in the sun – keep it as cool as possible.

7. Make sure there's no fruit near the bouquet, as gas from the fruit can make the flowers wilt faster.

ARRANGE THE SHORT-STEMMED DAHLIAS IN SMALL VASES OF VARYING HEIGHTS. IN THE VASES: 'PENHILL WATERMELON', 'CAFÉ AU LAIT', 'HENRIETTE', 'WINE EYED JILL', 'JOWEY WINNIE', 'SYLVIA' AND 'BABYLON BRONZE'.

Above left: Orange and coral-coloured dahlias look beautiful in clay urns.

Above: Yellow notes in your bouquets will create a joyous tutti-frutti feeling!

Left: Different stem lengths can make it hard to tie bouquets or arrange the flowers in vases. You can instead use flower fakirs and arrange your flowers on the small spikes. Make sure every stem is reaching the water.

Opposite: Dahlias also keep well in a water bowl. This works particularly well for flowers that have blown or broken off in a storm, or those that are fading.

MANY DAHLIAS WILL
STAY LOOKING FRESH
ON THE TABLE FOR A WHOLE
EVENING WITHOUT WATER.

'CAFÉ AU LAIT' DAHLIAS USUALLY HAVE SHORT STEMS, BUT THEY WORK WELL
ARRANGED ON A FAKIR TOGETHER WITH BLACK-EYED SUSAN 'SAHARA'.

Drying dahlias

Dried dahlias lose their rich colours but give way to
attractive muted hues. Cut off the flowers you wish
to dry, together with their stems, and hang them upside
down in a dark place that is dry and warm. The drying
process takes about a month. You can make a wreath
from the dried flowers, or you can store them in a large
jar. Or how about making a dahlia board by sticking
them onto a contrasting background, or creating a
dahlia 'tree'.

A MAGNOLIA BRANCH AND DRIED DAHLIAS.

ALLOW THE DAHLIAS TO DRY IN A DARK,
DRY PLACE.

Dahlia growers

In this chapter you will be introduced to three devoted dahlia growers from various parts of Sweden. Here they will share their top tips, from precultivation through to fertilizers and winter storage. There are many different ways of looking after your dahlias – experiment and see what works best for you!

Jan Ansbjer
Västergötland

How long have you been growing dahlias?
For over 20 years.

How did you start?
Dahlias were one of the many plants we started growing
in the early days.

Your winter-storage tips?
I keep them in plastic crates at 4–7°C (39–44°F) with
just the right degree of moisture.

Do you precultivate them indoors?
I've got fed up with starting them off indoors, because in
recent years June has been cold and windy, and the
plants I started early were slow getting going and didn't
mature that much earlier than those planted straight
into the soil outside. This is because our dahlia land is in
an exposed location with biting wind. I now have lilies,
which produce rich colours in June to July instead.

How often do you water them?
I loosen the soil after rain, so the moisture is retained.
Some summers I don't water them at all, but usually it's
just the once. If it's dry for a very long time I water them
three times.

How do you prepare the soil?
If it's dry enough in the autumn I turn the soil over once
we've lifted the dahlias. Once it's dried out in the spring
I turn the soil over again to warm it up and weaken the
overwintered weeds, and so the soil dries properly. After
a cold snap and rain we finally get dry, warm spring
weather. Then at the beginning of May I lay compost
and till it in, after which it's time to plant the dahlias.

'BREAK OUT'

YOU CAN ENJOY 350 TO 400 VARIETIES
OF DAHLIA IN NOSSEBRO.

Which fertilizers do you use?

Cow and horse manure. Also some garden compost. Over the past year the old compost had a low nitrogen content, so some of the land got a little chicken manure.

How many varieties do you have?

350 to 400.

Which varieties are on your wish list?

New ones from Dutch growers.

Your three favourite dahlias?

I admire the great variety in terms of shape and colour, so I can't choose, as many of them are brilliant in their own way.

How do you stop your dahlias falling prey to diseases and pests?

There are slugs and snails all over the garden, but I don't find them a great problem. I hoe the soil after rain in order to retain moisture and move the soil around, so no new weeds grow – but also so slugs and snails can't get around in the loose, dry soil. This means newly developed dahlia leaves are left in peace. Earwigs need a moist habitat in order to breed, and we don't have any moist stone walls or rotting pallet collars, and so have never had any problems with them. One year we had 15 or so dahlias with leafy gall, and last autumn we found three with this disease growing by a plum tree. We don't lift infected tubers, but we've tried overwintering them. The disease usually clears up during the winter, and doesn't return to the same place the following year. We've had some of our plantings for 20 years.

Instagram: @magnolianossebro

DAHLIAS AND SUNFLOWERS IN ONE OF MANY
DAHLIA BEDS IN A PRIVATE GARDEN IN MALMÖ.

Elin Thott
Skåne

How long have you been growing dahlias?
For around 10 years.

How did you start?
Can't remember where I got the inspiration, but I bought
six or seven tubers online from Holland the first time.
And then I just got more and more.

Where do you buy you tubers?
I basically waste money, buying from loads of different
places (with hefty freight charges) when I find varieties I
want. Mostly from Sweden and Holland, but from
Denmark and other European countries too. I also used
to buy from England.

Your winter-storage tip?
My top tip is spreading the risk and storing tubers in
several different ways. I dig most of mine up and maybe
halve them, so they easily fit into compost bags. I then
leave the bags open for a few days in the shed, so the
tubers can dry out, before packing the bags into removal
boxes, which have to be put somewhere as cool as
possible. I store particularly cherished varieties, or ones
that dry out more easily (long, thin tubers or loose
clumps of tubers), as single (divided) tubers, wrapped
in cling film.

Do you precultivate them indoors?
I now basically start all tubers indoors, as I use all my
flower beds and grow boxes for other things in the
winter and spring, as I want to get the dahlias going
before there's somewhere permanent for them. But I
used to put them straight into the soil outside, often as
early as at the beginning of April, and that went well too.

Do you divide dahlias in the autumn or the spring?
Advantages and disadvantages?
I divide them in both the autumn and the spring.

The tubers stored in cling film are washed and divided into individual tubers in the autumn. I sometimes divide the ones saved as clumps of tubers into smaller clumps, and then divide them into individual tubers in the spring. The disadvantage of dividing in the autumn is that the tubers more easily dry out if they're not kept close together (if they're not wrapped in cling film). The advantage of autumn division, on the other hand, is that the tubers then take up less space and are easier to handle.

How often do you water them?
I only water them when it's dry – apart from pots, which need water nearly every day in the summer.

How do you prepare the soil?
I fertilize all the beds with horse manure in the spring. When the dahlias are to be planted I dig a big hole, maybe mix in a little compost, and fertilize by adding a little bone meal and chicken fertilizer.

How many varieties do you have?
About 150.

Which varieties are on your wish list?
'Hollyhill Serenity', 'KA's Champagne' and 'Barbarry Gateway'.

Your three favourite dahlias?
'Bracken Rose', 'Staburadze' and 'Hamari Rose'.

What do you do to protect your dahlias against pests and diseases?
I combat slugs and snails by spreading Ferramol all over the garden several times a season, and I'm then left with just a few of these murderous creatures. I've found leafy gall a few times, luckily in pots, and have then immediately thrown the plants away.

'BRACKEN ROSE'

'HAMARI ROSE'

Which varieties are best for cut flowers?
'Sweet Love', 'American Dawn', 'Babylon Bronze' and 'Karma Prospero'.

Instagram: @tradgardstid

MARI MAGNUSSON BY THE
DAHLIA BED IN FRONT OF
HER GREENHOUSE.

Mari Magnusson
Uppland

'JOWEY WINNIE'

How long have you been growing dahlias?
For about three years.

How did you start?
Like everyone else, I fell in love with 'Café au Lait' dahlias
when they started popping up in my Instagram feed.

Your winter-storage tips?
I don't wash my dahlia roots, but just gently shake off
the soil and lay them in big open wooden boxes with a
little sawdust.

Do you precultivate them indoors?
Yes, in the hope they'll start flowering a few
weeks earlier.

Do you divide dahlias in the autumn or the spring?
In the spring, because in the autumn they're more
fragile and mould may develop on the cut surfaces.
In the spring I let the cut surfaces dry before planting
the newly divided tubers.

How often do you water them?
That depends on the weather, but once a week I give
them a good soak. Dahlias cope much better if you
mulch, as that greatly reduces evaporation.

How do you prepare the soil?
In the autumn I put down grass clippings and leaves,
and in the spring a thick layer of well decomposed
cow manure. In the summer I also mulch my dahlias
with several layers of grass clippings. This helps guard
against evaporation, provides nutrition and stops
weeds gaining a foothold.

Which fertilizers do you use?
Leachate from my bokashi soil factories, which I keep in big metal barrels with taps, and well decomposed cow manure, which I buy in the spring from farmers in the vicinity. I also use grass clippings, which provide slow nutrition.

How many varieties do you have?
Around 80.

Which varieties are on your wish list?
'Tyrell', 'Evanah' and 'Great Silence'.

Your three favourite dahlias?
'Penhill Dark Monarch', 'Labyrinth' and 'Café au Lait'.

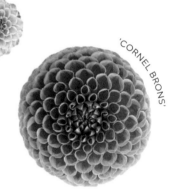

How do you stop your dahlias falling prey to pests and diseases?
I give the flowers the optimum conditions, such as good soil and regular watering, enabling them to better deal with diseases. It also helps to precultivate the tubers as it makes the plants grow larger and more resistant when they're planted out. I remove earwigs by hand and make corrugated-cardboard traps for them, which I then shake out over the compost, so the earwigs get to live there instead.

Which varieties do you think are the best for cut flowers?
Ball dahlias such as 'Jowey Winnie', 'Wine Eyed Jill', 'Cornel Brons' and 'Caitlin's Joy'.

Instagram: @anangelinmyhome

Index

Thank you

Huge thanks to Elin Thott for allowing me to photograph her lovely dahlia-filled garden in Malmö. And my heartfelt thanks to Jan Ansbjer at Magnolia, who received me with open arms and let me photograph all the hundreds of varieties in the fantastic display garden in Nossebro. Many thanks to Mari Magnusson who shared her joy in dahlias and her charming garden. Thank you to all three for your willingness to also be involved in the book. I also photographed dahlia varieties in the beautiful castle garden in Malmö – I'm grateful to you for that, Linnéa Dickson!

And I wish to thank Malte Heimerson, who worked on my photos, as well as the photographer Peter Carlsson for the pictures of me in the book. My thanks go to Marja Pennanen for the beautiful book design, and to Johanna Ekberg at Arena Bokförlag for her faith in my book concept and for being so incredibly nice to work with. And last but not least, thanks to my son Konrad for always being there for me, and to my partner Tim, who always says yes and collaborates in every project – from dahlia growing beds to an orangery, and now a whole dahlia farm at Österlen in Skåne!

First published as *Dahlia*. 222 sorter, odling, skötsel & inspiration in 2022 by Bokförlaget Arena, Sweden

This English language edition published in 2024 by Quadrille, an imprint of Hardie Grant Publishing

Quadrille
52–54 Southwark Street, London SE1 1UN
quadrille.com

Managing Director: Sarah Lavelle
Senior Commissioning Editor: Harriet Butt
Assistant Editor: Oreolu Grillo
Designer: Alicia House
Head of Production: Stephen Lang
Senior Production Controller: Katie Jarvis

Cataloguing in Publication Data: a catalogue record for this book is available from the British Library.

Text © Ulrika Grönlund 2024
Design © Quadrille 2024
Photography © Ulrika Grönlund 2024 except for page 5 and pages 136–137 Peter Carlsson 2024

ISBN 978 1 8378 3095 4
Printed in China using soy inks

FSC
www.fsc.org

MIX
Paper | Supporting responsible forestry
FSC™ C020056